GOD'S LOVE FOR YOU

Copyright © Anne Herridge, 2010. All rights reserved. No part of this book may be reproduced or transmitted in any form or by any means, electronic or mechanical, including photocopying, recording, or by any information storage and retrieval system, without permission in writing from the publisher.

Unless otherwise indicated, all Scripture quotations are taken from the Holy Bible, New Living Translation, copyright ©1996. Used by permission of Tyndale House Publishers, INC., Wheaton, Illinois 60189. All rights reserved.

Scripture quotation taken from the Amplified® Bible, Copyright © 1954, 1958, 1962, 1964, 1965, 1987 by The Lockman Foundation. Used by permission. (www.Lockman.org)

Millennial Mind Publishing
An imprint of American Book Publishing
5442 So. 900 East, #146
Salt Lake City, UT 84117-7204
www.american-book.com
Printed in the United States of America on acid-free paper.

God's Love for You
Designed by Jana Rade, design@american-book.com

Publisher's Note: American Book Publishing relies on the author's integrity of research and attribution; each statement has not been investigated to determine if it has been accurately made. The author and publisher specifically disclaim any responsibility for any liability, loss, or risk, personal or otherwise, which is incurred as a consequence, directly or indirectly, of the use and application of any of the contents of this book. In such situations where medical, legal, or other professional services may apply, please seek the advice of such professionals directly.

Library of Congress Cataloging-in-Publication Data
Herridge, Anne.
God's love for you / Anne Herridge.
 p. cm.
ISBN-13: 978-1-58982-571-0
ISBN-10: 1-58982-571-3
1. God (Christianity)--Love--Meditations. 2. God--Love--Biblical teaching--Meditations. I. Title.
BT140.H44 2009
231'.6--dc22
 2009045080

Special Sales
These books are available at special discounts for bulk purchases. Special editions, including personalized covers, excerpts of existing books, and corporate imprints, can be created in large quantities for special needs. For more information e-mail info@american-book.com.

GOD'S LOVE FOR YOU

ANNE HERRIDGE

For Stuart, Kimberley and Jonathan, who inspired this book.

For my Mum, Rita, who taught me much about God's love.

For my Dad, John. Thanks for all you have done for me.

God loves you all, and so do I.

FOREWORD

"How deep the Father's love for us; how vast beyond all measure." The words of this beautiful, thought-provoking hymn echoed in my mind as I read this book written by Anne Herridge. If you have ever felt overwhelmed by guilt, shame, loneliness, fear, or insecurity, then this book is for you. Anne's message is that God sees you just as you are and that He loves you so much more than you could ever imagine. Her words are tantalizing and true. They have reverberated throughout the universe since the beginning of time. The author weaves this love story in a way that will compel and draw you.

While you, the reader, may never have had the pleasure of meeting Anne, I am privileged to call her my friend. Anne has worked as a counselor in my church and has heard many stories of brokenness and alienation. I have been heartened to watch the way that she has used her skill and compassion to point people to the ultimate source of love and then to help them restore their own damaged relationships.

She does it once again through her writings. Pick up a cup of coffee, put up your feet, and let the words of this book inspire and move you. You will be drawn to God's tenderness. Anne knows of what she speaks. Countless lives have been immeasurably changed because of these timeless truths.

Sharon Gaetz
Mayor of Chilliwack
Former Pastor, SouthSide Church
Chilliwack, BC

God loves you. He loves you so much that He has left signs of His love all over nature.

For ever since the world was created, people have seen the earth and sky.
Through everything God made, they can clearly see his invisible qualities - his eternal power and divine nature.

Romans 1:20

God loves you and wants you to find Him. One of the ways He has chosen to reveal Himself to you is through nature. He has left clues all over the natural world that hint of His love for you, to show you what He is like. Consider the beauty of a sunset, the delicate sparkle of a dewdrop, the intricate details of a snowflake, the power of the wind and the cycle of the seasons that display continuous new life. God has made it simple to find Him. No matter what culture you are from, what language you speak, whether you are rich or poor, young or old, you can see and experience what God is like through the natural world.

His fingerprints are everywhere. On every leaf, every butterfly wing, every seashell, every grain of sand. He created the world as an expression of His love for you. Don't be too busy to notice the clues He has left. Stop and take a deep breath. God is nearer than you think, longing for you to see Him in and through the world He made for you.

God's Love for You

All nature speaks, like the flower, messages from God, the Father of the universe. – George Macdonald 1

If you look closely, you will see that God's heart of love is all around.

….unfailing love surrounds those who trust the Lord.

Psalm 32:10

Loneliness is said to be one of the biggest diseases of our time. You are not alone. The God who made you, chose you. He has a plan for you. He is standing with you every moment of each day, longing for you to know He is there, wanting you to know that He cares about you. Others might leave you, reject you, or withdraw their love from you. God's love surrounds you always. You may not feel it, but that doesn't mean it is not there. You mean so much to God. He made you and He knows you fully. He accepts you and loves you without condition. He cares about every detail of your life, more than you can know. The Bible says that He takes great delight in you and rejoices over you with singing (Zephaniah 3:17).

A mother may sing to her new baby, not just to comfort the baby and reassure him of her presence, but to express the indescribable love and joy she feels for her precious child. Sometimes the baby may seem unaware of his mother or father's presence. He may cry out, only to find that his loving parent was not very far away. He was not alone after all. He was simply unable to see his parent. Like babies and young children, we are often unaware that God's loving presence is with us all the time.

God's Love for You

.. be sure of this: I am with you always, even to the end of the age.
- Jesus (Matthew 28:20)

Anne Herridge

The words of a popular worship song say it well:

> *You dance over me*
> *While I am unaware*
> *You sing all around*
> *But I never hear the sound*

Lord, I'm amazed by You...how You love me

> *You paint the morning sky*
> *With miracles in mind*
> *My hope will always stand*
> *For You hold me in Your hand*

Lord, I'm amazed by You...how You love me

> *How wide, how deep*
> *How great is your love for me*
> *How wide, how deep*
> *How great is your love for me*

Lord, I'm amazed by You...how You love me
.
> *I'm amazed by You*
> *Lord, I'm amazed every day*
> *So amazed*
> *How You love me, Lord* 2

God's love for you is stronger than a rock.

*The Lord is my rock, my fortress, and my savior;
my God is my rock, in whom I find protection.*

Psalm 18:2

This world is not always a safe place to live. Life can be unpredictable and even dangerous at times. Even when life is good, people may let us down or surprise us with lack of commitment or weak friendship. We all need to feel safe. God designed us to feel secure, which is why insecurity and fear make us feel so vulnerable. What do you need to feel secure, safe, and protected? A baby bird feels safe under a mother's wing. A child feels safe in the lap of a loving parent. A soldier feels secure under the authority of a good commanding officer. A bank clerk feels secure knowing that a security guard is close by.

God wants to be your protector. Having made you His own, His desire is to be your guard, your shield, and your defender. The One who made the universe is a force to be reckoned with! He is described as being like a huge rock that cannot be moved or broken. He is like a shadow that is large enough to shield you from the burning heat of the sun, a fortress or garrison with all the resources and weapons necessary to defend you.

God's Love for You

God has promised to shelter and cover you like a bird shelters her young under her feathered wings. He has promised not to let your foot slip, to watch over you day and night, to be with you in trouble.

Nothing can distract or discourage Him from this task because you are His top priority. Imagine how it would feel to have someone who loves you, continually at your side. Someone who never sleeps, but who watches out for you, who walks ahead of you on the path to check for danger. Someone who advises you, defends you, and who is on your side. That Someone is God.

God invites us to choose to put ourselves under His authority. We must entrust our lives to Him in order to experience this protection and safety. If a soldier chooses to disregard his orders and fight alone in a battle, he is no longer under the protection of his squad. If a child fails to listen to a parent and touches a hot stove, he is no longer safe. If a driver chooses to teach himself to drive without the wisdom of an experienced instructor, he may end up in an accident.

In ancient times, it was possible for a king's subjects to travel with letters from the king to ensure safe passage through certain territories. In the same way, we can travel through this world with or without the King's protection. He is longing to travel with you. He wants you to know that His heart is for you, to shield, defend, and protect you.

The Lord says, "I will rescue those who love me. I will protect those who trust in my name." – Psalm 91:14

Just like the sky, his love for you is forever.

Give thanks to the God of heaven. His faithful love endures forever.

Psalm 136:26

Few things in life last forever. Many marriages no longer last a lifetime. Friendships come and go, employment is not guaranteed. In an ever changing world, there seems to be very little that remains the same. God is unchanging. He will not change the way He loves you. He will not change His mind about you, ever. He will never run out of love for you. Just as the sky appears to have no end to a child's eyes, but continues on forever, so it is with God's love for you. His love is endless. You are secure. He will never run out of kindness, mercy, grace, or commitment to you. His plans for you are forever plans. He designed you with eternity in mind. His plan was, and still is, that you would live in a love relationship with Him forever.

Your life here on Earth is only the beginning. It is just temporary. If life here is uncomfortable, know that you have comfort coming. If you have missed opportunities or have dreams that have not been realized, know that God has greater dreams for you. It is never too late to realize dreams when there is an eternal plan for your life. If you have lost loved ones, take comfort from the fact that you will spend eternity with them. Try not to allow this temporary life to discourage or distract you. There is hope for your future.

God's Love for You

As you journey through this life, know that the God of history, the One who created Time and Space and who is above all physical and natural laws, is there ahead of you, knowing the content and length of your days. He is by your side. He has got your back. His love and Presence surround you and He has an eternal destiny for you.

It's wonderful to climb the liquid mountains of the sky.
Behind me and before me is God and I have no fears.
- Helen Keller 3

God's thoughts about you outnumber the grains of sand on the seashore.

How precious are your thoughts about me, O God.
They cannot be numbered!
I can't even count them;
they outnumber the grains of sand!

Psalm 139: 17, 18

When you are in love with someone, you think about that person all the time. You dream about them. You may be distracted by thoughts of them. You love everything about them, even the bad things! Did you know that God is in love with you? In fact, He is crazy about you! He thought of you before you were born. He planned the day of your birth. He has planned from the beginning of time that you should be born into the world at this time and in this generation. The Bible says that you were not born because of human decision, but because of God. It was His decision and will that you should be here.

You may not think about God all the time, but He is thinking of you. He loves to think about you. He thinks about you through the night as you sleep and as you wake to each new day. He thinks about you all day long, even when you forget He is there. The Bible says that his Son, Jesus, is praying and interceding for you in heaven. You are being prayed for right now as you read these words.

God's Love for You

How does it feel to know that the Creator of the Universe has you foremost in His thoughts? What are His thoughts about you? Perhaps you are afraid that when He thinks of you, it is only with regret or disappointment. This is not true. His thoughts about you are full of pride and joy. His plans for you are for peace, prosperity and hope, not harm or disaster. He believes in you. He is patiently seeking the best for you. He is committed to you one hundred percent.

How His heart longs for you to know that He cares. You have Someone on your side. He cares when you have a bad day. His thoughts are compassionate and caring toward you. He rejoices with you when your day is good. If you are sad, He is weeping with you, feeling your pain.

We often worry about what other people think of us. All that really matters is what God thinks about us. His thoughts are motivated by love.

For I know the thoughts and plans that I have for you, says the Lord, thoughts and plans for welfare and peace and not for evil, to give you hope in your final outcome. - Jeremiah 29:11 (Amplified Bible)

You are engraved on the palms of God's hand.
He will never forget you.

See, I have written your name on the palms of my hands.

Isaiah 49:16

It is impossible for God to forget you. The Bible says that He has engraved or imprinted a picture of you on each of His hands. Engraving is permanent. It cannot be changed or removed. Sometimes people have the name of someone they love tattooed onto their body. They may have jewelry engraved with another person's name. God's commitment to you is so permanent that He went a step further and had both His hands engraved with your name. Unlike us, He does not change His mind about loving us or regret this decision. He has promised never to forget you. People may forget about you, but God does not.

Couples often hold hands when they are in love. Parents hold the tiny hands of their newborn babies, marveling at the miniature fingers and wondering what those little hands will do when they are grown. They long to protect those hands and hope that they never experience pain or suffering.

The hand of the one you love is so precious that sometimes you don't want to let it go. It represents commitment, safety, and love. God never wants to let go of your hand, but sometimes, like children who want independence from a parent, we slip our hand out of His grip.

God's Love for You

God's hands reflect His heart. If you could look at His hands, you would see your name. His hands created you and brought you into the world. It was His hands that first held your tiny fingers, already knowing the hard work your hands would be used for, the pain your hands might suffer, and the beautiful things your hands would create. With your hand in His, you can accomplish great things.

His hands not only protect and nurture; they mould and transform His creation into beauty. Just as the potter takes a piece of lifeless clay and works it into an exquisite vase, or the carpenter takes a piece of wood and creates a beautiful piece of furniture, so God can form and change you into the magnificent man or woman He designed you to be.

His hands are large enough to hold all of His creation. They also bear the scars of two nails that were used to pin Him to a cross when He suffered and died for you, so that you could find your way back to Him and take hold of His hand once again.

Because God is so free from stain, so loving, so unselfish, so good, so altogether what he wants us to be, so holy, therefore all his works declare him in beauty. His fingers can touch nothing but to mould it into loveliness...
- George MacDonald 4

You are worth more to God than the most beautiful flower

And if God cares so wonderfully for flowers that are here today and thrown into the fire tomorrow, he will certainly care for you.
Luke 12:28

A common complaint today is that people do not care for one another. Busy western culture has created a society where there is little time for caring for the needs of others. But God cares about you. You are valuable. You are worth caring about. You are meant to be here. God made you. His work is wonderful. God never makes mistakes. You are of great worth and value because God has made you in His own image. You have holy DNA! You have been wired for significance. You have a Divine streak in you that God wants to cultivate into something beautiful. In prayer and worship, we often declare that God is worthy, but He also wants to whisper to you that *you* are worthy. You have great worth because He suffered and died for you and bought you new life.

The Bible tells the story of a Shepherd leaving ninety-nine sheep to find just one who was lost and separated from the others. It tells the story of a man who found a pearl of such great worth that he sold everything he had to buy the field where the pearl was hidden. You are of tremendous worth to God. He gave up everything for you, so that you can know

God's Love for You

you are loved and cared for. He gave the life of his Son, Jesus, for you. The Creator of the universe was willing to die for you. He did so, because His heart's desire is for a relationship with you.

Not only does He care for you, but He sees beauty within you. You are more beautiful and valuable than the most exquisite flower or sunset in creation. The world sees beauty in temporary terms, valuing youth, wealth, fashion, and body shape or size. God sees the beauty within you. He sees the potential He has given you. He sees the end result. He sees the gifts He has given to you. He says He has placed treasure inside you. Even if you don't see it or believe it is there.

Because of your tremendous value and worth, God has promised to meet all your needs. Love does not abandon its most cherished possession.

Give all your worries and cares to God, for he cares about you.
-1 Peter 5:7

Even when you are feeling prickly, God still loves you.

...love covers a multitude of sins.

1 Peter 4:8

We all have 'prickly' days or moments when we fail to show our best side or fail to love others as we should. We wonder how God can love us when we often let Him down so much. But God loves you even on bad days. He knows you better than you know yourself. He loves every part of you, the good, bad, and the ugly parts. God is never disappointed with you. To be disappointed means that you expect something or someone to turn out differently. God already knows how you are going to turn out. In the Bible, He says that every day of your life was known to Him, even before one of those days came to pass. He already knows how you will behave today, tomorrow and next week. He loves you all the same. His love for you is based on His character, not on your behavior. His love for you is without condition.

Not many people would touch a cactus plant. They are spiky, painful, and not very pretty. Yet, many cactus plants have the ability to bloom and produce beautiful flowers. Just as God can bring beauty from something so prickly and unattractive, He can see the beauty in you. He can help you to blossom and become the person He made you to be. He loves you in spite of your faults. He can bring beauty out of your prickles.

Unconditional love is never based upon the merit of the one receiving it; it is based upon the loving nature of the one giving it - Jack Frost, Shiloh Place Ministries 5

Though your heart is not always pure, God's heart is pure towards you.

Then I will sprinkle clean water on you, and you will be clean.

Ezekiel 36:25

You have made mistakes. There are days when you struggle with wrong thoughts and make bad choices. You may find it hard to believe that God can love you when your heart and mind are far from pure. But God's heart is pure towards you. His love is pure – undiluted, unconditional, untainted. Although you are tainted and stained by your mistakes, God's love is able to wash you clean. The Bible says that He has covered our sins and blotted them out, just as thick clouds cover the sky, or snow covers the ground and erases roads, paths, and landmarks.

Graffiti is a problem in many cities. It stains and defaces property and can be hard to clean. There is a product that can be applied to these surfaces now which prevents paint or markers from sticking to the surface and staining them. When this coating is applied, graffiti can simply be cleaned away, leaving no traces. In the same way, if you admit to your mistakes and bring them to God, He can erase them. He is the best cleaner in the world!

God's Love for You

God's heart is not only pure, but trusting. He loves you so much that He is willing to give you endless opportunities. He is not only a God of second chances, but third, fourth, fifth, sixth, and ninety-sixth chances! He believes in forgiving continually. He keeps no record of wrongs. He sees the best in you even when you don't. He believes in you, even when you don't believe in yourself.

Accept God's forgiveness and His offer to cleanse your soul. Know that He has nothing but love and understanding for you in His heart.

...he saved us, not because of the righteous things we had done, but because of his mercy. He washed away our sins, giving us a new birth and new life through the Holy Spirit.
– Titus 3:5

God has given his heart to you. Will you give yours to Him?

You must love the Lord your God with all your heart, all your soul, and all your mind.

Matthew 22:37

God made you for Himself. He created you in love. He intended you to enjoy a loving relationship with Him. It is only when you are secure in the knowledge of His love, that you can love others and live effectively. It has been said that each person has a "God shaped" hole inside – a place deep in the soul that only God can fill. Yet, if God does not fill this hole in the soul, we look for other things or people to fill it. Like a ship off course, we often spend time and energy running in the wrong direction, pursuing things to make us feel fulfilled, whole, or loved. Yet none of the things we pursue satisfy our hungry souls for very long.

We have all given our heart to something or someone. It has been said that whatever our heart clings to, is really our God. Whatever we have given our heart, our time, our energy or our money to, is the thing we value most. We are in danger of being so occupied with pursuing created things, that we forget the Creator Himself.

God's Love for You

God has asked that we give our heart to Him because He has designed our hearts for Him. Only a God-shaped peg can fit perfectly into a God-shaped heart. He has made us this way. He does not want to control us or have us as a puppet on a string. He wants the best for us! Nobody knows His creation better than the Creator Himself. If a man designs and builds an engine, he is best qualified to fix it, if it needs repair. If a gardener plants a garden, he is best qualified to advise which plants thrive perfectly in which part of the garden. If your heart has been designed for a special purpose and relationship, and that relationship is not intact, your heart will be restless, even homeless, until it is fulfilled the way it was designed to be.

God has your best interests at heart. He knows you better than you know yourself. He knows how to satisfy and fulfill you. He has promised that if you give your heart to Him, life will go well. It is His deepest desire that life goes well for you.

God's heart is for you. His heart is tender, even vulnerable, yearning for you to find Him. Will you allow Him into your life? Is your heart restless? Is something missing? Will you trust Him with your heart and give it back to Him?

…you have made us and drawn us to yourself, and our heart is unquiet until it rests in you - Saint Augustine 6

PRAYER

If you would like to give your heart to God and to know him better, you may find the following prayer helpful:

God, thank you for your love for me. Thank you for watching over my life, even though I have been unaware of You. Please forgive me for not always seeing evidence of Your love around me. Thank you, that You have an eternal plan and purpose for me. I know there is hope for my future. Thank you for the gifts you have given me. Thank you for seeing the best in me, even when I have not. Please forgive me for those times when my heart has not been pure. Forgive me for not realizing that You are my heart's true home.

I long to know you better, God. I want to live my life for You. I choose to live under Your authority and protection. Thank you that Your heart is for me. I give my heart to You, and invite You into my life. Amen.

At the cross God wrapped his heart in flesh and blood and let it be nailed to the cross for our redemption – E. Stanley Jones 7

Notes

1. George Macdonald, *Wisdom To Live By – Nuggets of Insight from all collected works.* Page 63. Copyright 1996 Sunrise Books Publishers, Eureka, California 95501. A Division of One Way, Ltd. Used with permission.

2. **Amazed**
   Words and Music by Jared Anderson
   © 2003 Vertical Worship Songs/ASCAP
   c/o Integrity Media, Inc., 1000 Cody Road, Mobile, AL 36695
   All Rights Reserved. International Copyright Secured. Used by Permission

3. Helen Keller, at age 74, on flight around the world, news reports of 5 February 1955.

4. George MacDonald, *Wisdom To Live By – Nuggets of Insight from all collected works.* Page 62. Copyright 1996 Sunrise Books Publishers, Eureka, California

95501. A Division of One Way, Ltd. Used with permission.

5. Jack Frost, *Experiencing Father's Embrace,* Destiny Image Inc. 2002
   Used with permission from Shiloh Place Ministries, PO Box 5, Conway, SC 29528; *www.shilohplace.org (Ph. 843-365-8990)*

6. St Augustine, *The Confessions,* Vintage Spiritual Classics 1998.
   A Division of Random House, Inc. New York Copyright 1997 Augustinian Heritage Institute. Maria Boulding, OSB., Translator, John E. Rotelle, OSA., Editor. Used with permission.

7. E. Stanley Jones, Source obtained from the internet, BrainyQuote.com.
   Accessed May 2008. Note: the author has been unable to trace a more accurate source for this quotation. If any reader knows the origin of this quotation, please let the author know so that copyright may be acknowledged in any reprint of *God's Love For You.*

8. All photographs copyright © of Jadestone Photographic Arts., P.P.A.B.C.'s Photographer of the Year 2007 and Professional Photographers of Canada Best in Class (Press) Photographer 2008 Chilliwack, B.C. *www.jadestonephoto.com (Ph. 604-854-0502).* Used with permission.

Acknowledgments

My grateful thanks to American Book Publishing Group for giving this first time author an opportunity to be published. You truly are the "friend down there" who knows the best way forward. I especially want to thank Dilna Khory for working so patiently and diligently with me on the manuscript, and all the staff at ABP who have contributed to, or shepherded me through the publishing process.

Special thanks also go to Sharon Gaetz who, despite a very busy schedule, was willing to write the Foreword, and to her husband, Jim. You are both wonderful pastors and leaders. You have taught me much about God's love for His people.

I also want to thank Shiloh Place Ministries (Destiny Image Inc.) for all the work that you do for the Kingdom. Your Ministry has been hugely inspiring and encouraging not only to me, but to many of my counseling clients.

I would also like to thank my husband and children for their constant patience and encouragement as the book took shape.

Grateful thanks also go to Joan Derish of Jadestone Photographic Arts, not only for the beautiful images she produced for the book, but also for her wisdom and professionalism throughout the project.

Last, but by no means least, I want to express my deepest appreciation to all the friends in my life who have shown God's love and heart for me. I would love to name each one of you, but there simply would not be room on the page! Thank you for your prayers, wisdom, encouragement, and laughter. May you come to know even more of God's love for you.

ABOUT THE AUTHOR

Anne Herridge has worked in pastoral care and counseling for many years, having trained with CWR in Farnham, UK. She now lives in Chilliwack, BC, where she is involved in counseling and prayer ministry at Southside Church.

In her spare time she enjoys exploring the beautiful BC outdoors with her husband and children.

www.anneherridge.com